D1244157

ABIGAIL BRESLIN

Amie Jane Leavitt

Mitchell Lane
PUBLISHERS

P.O. Box 196
Hockessin, Delaware 19707
Visit us on the web: www.mitchelllane.com
Comments? email us: mitchelllane@mitchelllane.com

Printing   1   2   3   4   5   6   7   8   9

A Robbie Reader
Contemporary Biography

Abigail Breslin	Albert Pujols	Alex Rodriguez
Aly and AJ	Amanda Bynes	Ashley Tisdale
Brenda Song	Brittany Murphy	Charles Schulz
Dakota Fanning	Dale Earnhardt Jr.	David Archuleta
Demi Lovato	Donovan McNabb	Drake Bell & Josh Peck
Dr. Seuss	Dwayne "The Rock" Johnson	Dylan & Cole Sprouse
Eli Manning	Emily Osment	Hilary Duff
Jaden Smith	Jamie Lynn Spears	Jesse McCartney
Jimmie Johnson	Johnny Gruelle	Jonas Brothers
Jordin Sparks	LeBron James	Mia Hamm
Miley Cyrus	Miranda Cosgrove	Raven-Symone´
Selena Gomez	Shaquille O'Neal	Story of Harley-Davidson
Syd Hoff	Tiki Barber	Tom Brady
Tony Hawk		

Library of Congress Cataloging-in-Publication Data
Leavitt, Amie Jane.
   Abigail Breslin / by Amie Jane Leavitt.
      p. cm. — (A Robbie reader)
   Includes bibliographical references and index.
   ISBN 978-1-58415-759-5 (library bound)
   1. Breslin, Abigail, 1996– —Juvenile literature. 2. Actors—United States—
Biography—Juvenile literature. I. Title.
   PN2287.B6855L43 2009
   791.4302'8092—dc22
   [B]
                                                                        2009006313

ABOUT THE AUTHOR: Amie Jane Leavitt is an accomplished author and photographer. She graduated from Brigham Young University as an education major and has since taught all subjects and grade levels in both private and public schools. She is an adventurer who loves to travel the globe in search of interesting story ideas and beautiful places to capture on film. She has written dozens of books for kids, has contributed to online and print media, and has worked as a consultant, writer, and editor for numerous educational publishing and assessment companies. Amie enjoys writing about people who are achieving their dreams. For this reason, she particularly enjoyed researching and writing this book on Abigail Breslin.

TABLE OF CONTENTS

Words in **bold** type can be found in the glossary.

In *Little Miss Sunshine*, Abby starred with a cast of famous actors.
Greg Kinnear (left) played the part of her father, Richard Hoover.
Toni Collette (center) played the role of her mother, Sheryl Hoover.
All of the cast members attended a party in New York in July 2006
after the New York City premiere of the film.

A Big Night at Sundance

Abigail Breslin was enjoying the film in the crowded Park City, Utah, theater, but she was also a little embarrassed. She often feels that way when she sees herself on the big screen. Over a thousand people had waited eagerly for the Sundance Film Festival's opening night film. This year, 2006, it was *Little Miss Sunshine*, and Abby was the movie's main actress.

When the film finally ended, the people in the audience jumped to their feet. At first, Abby was startled. When people jumped up like that in her hometown of New York, it was usually because there was an emergency like a fire. But that's not what was happening in Utah. As soon

Abby won many awards for her performance in *Little Miss Sunshine*, including Best Young Actress at the 12th Annual Critics' Choice Awards in Santa Monica, California.

as the crowd jumped up, they started clapping and cheering for the movie. They loved it!

After it premiered at Sundance, *Little Miss Sunshine* was bought by a larger company. It was then shown in theaters around the world. Very few people said anything negative about the film. Critics were especially positive about Abby's performance.

A year later, on January 23, 2007, Abby's mom and brother Spencer woke her up early one morning. They had exciting news. She'd been nominated for an Oscar! Also called an Academy Award, this is one of the highest awards that an actor can win. And Abby was still just a kid.

You'd think this success would change Abby, but it didn't. "I still have to make my bed and clean my room," she told *Tribute Canada* in July 2007.

Abby's story doesn't end with *Little Miss Sunshine*. It doesn't start there, either. It actually began ten years earlier in a hospital in Manhattan.

Abby's older brother, Spencer, is also an actor. The two siblings have performed together in several movies.

Thumb Wars

Abigail Breslin was born on April 14, 1996, in New York City. Michael and Kim Breslin already had two children. But this new baby, whom they would call Abby, would be their only daughter.

Abby's older brother, Ryan, was born in 1985. Spencer was born in 1992.

When Abby was one, Spencer was cast in his first commercial. He was only three at the time—an age that would later prove to be a magic one for the Breslins. After the commercial, Spencer was cast in roles on television. His big break came in 2000 when he performed with Bruce Willis in Disney's *The Kid*.

When Abby turned three, she followed in her brother's footsteps by appearing in a television commercial. And just like her brother, she didn't stop. "I just kept doing it, and I liked it," she told *Entertainment News* several years later.

When children work as actors, they need to have a manager who will watch out for them. Abby's mother is her manager. She always makes sure Abby is treated fairly.

When Abby was six, she was cast in the alien movie *Signs*. Talk show hosts Regis & Kelly asked her if she was scared during filming. "I actually didn't think it was that scary because when we were shooting it we didn't have the aliens in it," she said. Besides, she was having too much fun on the set. When they weren't acting, she and Joaquin Phoenix (wah-KEEN FEE-niks) would play thumb wars. "I always won but I think it's because he kind of let me win because I was little," she said, laughing.

Abby's mom is her manager, so she has a big say in what roles Abby plays. Abby told a *Time* magazine reporter: "My mom reads the script first, and then she tells me if I can read it or not. If I can, I'll read, and I'll see if it's somebody I would want to know."

Signs was a great beginning for Abby. In 2003, she was nominated for an award for her performance.

11

As an actor, Abby is often asked to help at special events. In 2006, she was asked to help present some awards at the MTV Video Music Awards with Fergie of the Black Eyed Peas.

Little Miss Actress

While kids her age were playing in the schoolyard, Abby was busy making movies. From 2004 to 2006, she was in ten films. In three of them (*Princess Diaries 2, Raising Helen,* and *The Santa Clause 3*), Spencer performed with her. Abby also had television roles. She appeared in **episodes** (EH-pih-sohdz) of *Grey's Anatomy, What I Like About You*, and *Ghost Whisperer*.

Shortly after *Signs*, Abby **auditioned** (aw-DIH-shund) for a part in the independent film *Little Miss Sunshine*. She was only six years old, but it took three years for the producers to fund the movie. Finally, in 2005, filming began.

In 2004, Jay Leno interviewed Abby and Spencer on *The Tonight Show*. Since it was close to Christmas, Abby brought Jay a gingerbread house she had made. Throughout the segment, Jay and Spencer kept teasing Abby about having a boyfriend. Every time they brought it up, she would repeat, "I do not have a boyfriend," and the audience would laugh.

Little Miss Sunshine was filmed in the Southwest. Abby had to wear a padded leotard under her clothes to make her look chubby. "It was so hot and sweaty and uncomfortable," she told *Daily Variety* in February 2007.

The movie is about a family who is going to a children's beauty contest. Even though the movie is about a family, it isn't a movie for kids.

An *Entertainment Weekly* reporter once asked Alan
Arkin (above) what he thought about a particular scene in
Little Miss Sunshine when Abby had to cry and be very
emotional. He said, "She didn't talk to a soul about it. She
doesn't have an [acting] coach. She refused to talk to
her mother. She wouldn't talk to me at all that morning.
She was concentrating on what she wanted to do. It was
sensational."

CHAPTER THREE

In February 2007, Abby helped present one of the
Academy Awards with fellow actor Jaden Smith.
Jaden is the son of Will and Jada Pinkett Smith.
Abby would later star with Jaden's sister, Willow, in
Kit Kittredge.

During some of the scenes, Abby had to listen to music on a CD player so that she couldn't hear the adults' conversations.

Many people loved Abby's performance, even her fellow actors. "It's like you're working with someone who's been in the business as long as you have," Alan Arkin told *Entertainment Weekly* in February 2007. Arkin played Abby's grandfather in the movie. He has been acting since the 1960s.

Little Miss Sunshine turned out to be an important step in Abby's career. After all, she was nominated for an Oscar for it! She was the fourth youngest actor to have been nominated for one.

The Academy Awards was a lot of fun for Abby. She wore fancy jewelry and a dress made just for her. She even met some of her favorite stars. The next day, she went with her family to Disneyland! When an NPR reporter asked her which she was more excited about, Abby said, "Both. It's too hard to choose."

Abby enjoyed playing in *Kit Kittredge* for many reasons. One of those was because she learned a lot about history and how things used to be. "Believe it or not, the thing that threw me the most was using a typewriter," she said. "I had to use one in a couple of scenes, so I was sitting down to get ready to use it, and I asked, 'Where's the screen?'"

Abigail Mania

Theaters seemed to have "Abigail Mania" in 2008. Almost as soon as her *No Reservations* was shown in 2007, Abby was in three more movies: *Definitely, Maybe; Kit Kittredge: An American Girl;* and *Nim's Island.*

Abby enjoyed working in all of those, but she was particularly excited to be cast in *Nim's Island.* She got to do many things she'd never tried before. "I'd never really done an action-y kind of adventure movie before," she told *Girls' Life* in April 2008. In a Reuters interview, she said, "I got to work with sea lions and bearded dragon lizards and the pelican. I learned how to make them do tricks."

Abby's role in *Nim's Island* was a perfect fit for her. She loved working with the animals and getting an opportunity to help train them.

In one scene, she gets to ride on the back of a sea lion. She also takes a trip down a zip line, which she compared to gliding through the air "like a flying squirrel." Since swimming is one of her favorite sports, she really enjoyed her time in the water. "I learned how to do duck dives, how to hold my breath under water, and even how to scream under water," she said.

Kit Kittredge: An American Girl was another film in which she played the lead. She collects American Girl dolls, and Kit is actually one of her favorites. This was also Abby's first "period movie"—a movie set in a particular time period—and she really enjoyed it. "I got to learn so much about history in a very real way," she told *People* in September 2007.

Since the story takes place during the **Great Depression**, Abby interviewed her grandmother, who had been a kid at that time. "She told me all these things about bread lines, how hard things were. . . . All those people struggling to just have enough to eat," Abby told the *Orlando Sentinel* in July 2008. She also told *Entertainment News* that she really loved the message of the film. It's "about family and friends pulling together in hard times. This movie shows that if you go through hard times, you can still pull through."

Abby helps out with many different charities. She is particularly attracted to charities that help animals.

An All-American Girl

Abby may be a successful actor, but she's also just a kid. She wants to be a **veterinarian** (veh-trih-NAYR-ee-un) when she grows up. Her favorite animals, besides her pets (two cats, two dogs, and a turtle), are elephants and orangutans.

Abby enjoys talking on the phone, having sleepovers with her friends and cousins, shopping, and listening to music. The Jonas Brothers are her favorite band.

Abby is home schooled. Her favorite subject is reading, and *Anne of Green Gables* is her favorite book. "I like how Anne acts," she told *People* in 2007. "She's always getting herself in trouble." Abigail also likes art and writing. "I like to write poems about pets and stuff like that," she told *Daily Variety* in 2008.

Abby likes to cook. She even went to the French **Culinary** (KYOO-lih-nayr-ee) Institute to prepare for *No Reservations*. In July 2007, she made her great-great grandmother's nutmeg cookies on the *Martha Stewart Show*. In addition to cookies, Abby also likes to make fried peanut butter and jelly sandwiches.

Grandma Stafford's Nutmeg Cookies Recipe

Ingredients
* Unsalted butter, for baking sheet
* I cup sugar
* 1/2 cup vegetable shortening
* 2 large eggs
* 2 cups all-purpose flour
* 1/2 teaspoon baking soda
* 1/2 teaspoon ground nutmeg
* 1/4 teaspoon salt
* I cup buttermilk

Makes 3 dozen

Directions
1. Preheat oven to 350 degrees. Butter a baking sheet and set aside.
2. In the bowl of an electric mixer fitted with the paddle attachment, beat together sugar and shortening until well combined. Add eggs, mixing until incorporated.
3. In a large bowl, sift together flour, baking soda, nutmeg, and salt. With the mixer running, add flour, alternating with buttermilk and beginning and ending with flour; mix until well combined.
4. Using a tablespoon, drop dough onto prepared baking sheet and transfer to oven. Bake until edges are slightly brown, about 15 minutes.

In March 2008, Abby became an honorary member of the Girl Scouts. When asked if she would sell the cookies, she said, "I'm afraid if I starting selling them, I'd start eating them."

You'd probably think that Abby can buy anything she wants, but that's not how it is. Just like many other kids, Abby gets an allowance: $12 a week at 12 years old. The rest of her money goes into a **trust fund** for when she's an adult.

Abby loves helping others. She volunteers at many functions, especially those for people with illnesses and for animals in trouble. While shooting *Nim's Island*, Abby earned money for **charity** (CHAH-rih-tee) at the same time. Whenever anyone on the set would say a bad word, she would make them put $2 into a jar. By the end, she had collected over $150. She gave it to an **organization** (or-gah-nih-ZAY-shun) that protects animals.

Because of all the work that Abby does for others, she was given the Young Heroes

Abby accepts the Young Heroes Award for being a good role model. At the event, she said her role model is actress Meryl Streep.

Award in 2008 by the Big Brothers Big Sisters program of Los Angeles. They said it was because "she is a positive role model for young people."

Abby has not had a typical childhood, but she has definitely enjoyed acting. "I've been really lucky. I like getting to be somebody else all the time and getting to travel," she told a *Reuters* reporter in 2008. When asked what kinds of roles she'd like to play in the future, she mentions more period pieces like the one she played in *Kit Kittredge*. "I would like to play Helen Keller and Lady Jane Grey," she told *Los Angeles Magazine* in June 2008.

Hopefully, for all of us moviegoers, Abby's sunshiny personality will still be on the big screen for many more years to come. Don't leave acting to become a veterinarian too soon, Abby!

CHRONOLOGY

1996 Abigail Breslin is born on April 14.

1999 She gets her first job—a part in a Toys R Us commercial.

2002 She plays the role of Bo Hess in *Signs*, Josie in an episode of *What I Like About You*, and Kayla Adams in *Hack*.

2003 She is nominated for Best Performance in a Feature Film by a Young Actress Age Ten or Under by the Young Artist Awards.

2004 She performs in *Chestnut: Hero of Central Park; Keane; The Princess Diaries 2;* and *Raising Helen;* and in episodes of *Law and Order* and *NCIS*.

2005 She performs in the made-for-television movie *Family Plan*.

2006 *Little Miss Sunshine* premieres at the Sundance Film Festival. She performs in *Santa Clause 3; Imaginary Friend; The Ultimate Gift;* and *Air Buddies*. She also performs in episodes of the *Ghost Whisperer* and *Grey's Anatomy*. She wins the Best Actress Award at the Tokyo Film Festival.

2007 She performs in *No Reservations* with Catherine Zeta Jones. She is nominated for an Oscar for the Best Performance by an Actress in a Supporting Role. She wins a Young Artist Award for Best Performance in a Feature Film by a Young Actress Age Ten or Under. She wins a Critics Choice Award for Best Young Actress. She wins a Screen Actors Guild Award for Outstanding Performance by a Cast in a Motion Picture.

2008 She performs in *Definitely, Maybe; Nim's Island;* and *Kit Kittredge: An American Girl*. She is nominated for a Young Artist Award for Best Performance in a Feature Film for a Leading Young Actress. She is nominated for a Teen Choice Award. She is named the Female Star of Tomorrow by the ShoWest Convention. She is given the Young Heroes Award by the Big Brothers Big Sisters of Los Angeles.

2009 She performs in *My Sister's Keeper, Zombieland,* and *Quantum Quest.* She is cast in *The Wild Bunch; Rango; Rape: A Love Story;* and *Dear Eleanor.*

FILMOGRAPHY

2010 *Rape: A Love Story*
2009 *Zombieland*
  The Wild Bunch (voice)
  Quantum Quest: A Cassini Space Odyssey (voice)
  My Sister's Keeper
  Dear Eleanor
2008 *Kit Kittredge: An American Girl*
  Nim's Island
  Definitely, Maybe
2007 *No Reservations*
2006 *Little Miss Sunshine*
  Air Buddies (voice)
  The Santa Clause 3: The Escape Clause
  The Ultimate Gift
2006 *Imaginary Friend*
2005 *Family Plan* (TV)
2004 *Chestnut: Hero of Central Park*
  Keane
  The Princess Diaries 2: Royal Engagement
  Raising Helen
2002 *Signs*

TV Shows

2006 *Grey's Anatomy* (1 episode)
  Ghost Whisperer (1 episode)
2004 *Navy NCIS: Naval Criminal Investigative Service*
    (1 episode)
  Law & Order: Special Victims Unit (1 episode, 2004)
2002 *What I Like About You* (1 episode)
  Hack (1 episode)

29

FIND OUT MORE

Articles

"Abigail Breslin." *Girls' Life*, April/May 2008, Vol. 14, Issue 5, p. 33.

"BIG Adventure." *Scholastic News*–Edition 5/6; April 14, 2008, Vol. 76, Issue 21, p. 8.

Dillard, Christiana. "Climbing to Success." *Weekly Reader News*–Edition 3; April 25, 2008, Vol. 77, Issue 26, p. 2-2.

Works Consulted

"CLIPS." *Hollywood Reporter*, International Edition; October 24, 2008, Vol. 407, Issue 5, pp. 3–8.

Dawson, Angela. "Breslin's Charm No Fluke." *Entertainment News*, June 26, 2008.

Debruge, Peter. "Supporting Actress: How We Got Here." *Daily Variety*, February 16, 2007, Vol. 294 Issue 36, p. A11.

Dougherty, Margot. "Abigail Breslin." *Los Angeles Magazine*, June 2008, Vol. 53 Issue 6, p. 121.

Hays, Holly. "Gerard Butler Has a Way with Women." *Redbook*, April 2008, Vol. 210, Issue 4, p. 43.

McCarthy, Ellen. "Abigail Breslin's Inquiring Mind Wants to Know." *Washington Post*, July 27, 2007.

Moore, Roger. "Despite Her Stardom, Abigail Breslin Remains All 'American Girl.' " *Orlando Sentinel*, July 4, 2008.

Serjeant, Jill. "Work Is Bundle of Fun for Little Miss Breslin." Reuters. April 1, 2008.

Setoodeh, Ramin. "Isn't She Just a Doll?" *Newsweek*; June 23, 2008, Vol. 151, Issue 25, p. 67.

"Talking with Abigail Breslin." *Time*, April 14, 2008. Vol. 171, Issue 15, p. 24.

Vary, Adam B. "Abigail Breslin." *Entertainment Weekly*, February 2, 2007, Issue 918/919, p. 54.

On the Internet

"Abigail Breslin–Fried Peanut Butter and Jelly." Fox 8 Clevelend. http://www.fox8.com/wjw-abigailbreslinfriedpeanut-6274491,0,3071054.story

An, Vickie. "Lights! Cameras! Animals!" *Time for Kids*. World Report, April 4, 2008. http://www.timeforkids.com/TFK/teachers/wr/article/0,27972,1726366,00.html

GLOSSARY

auditioned (aw-DIH-shund)—Tried out for a part in a play, movie, or other type of performance.

charity (CHAH-rih-tee)—A group or organization that helps people or animals in need.

culinary (KYOO-lih-nayr-ee)—Relating to the kitchen or to cooking.

episode (EH-pih-sohd)—An event that is part of a series of events, like a show in a television series.

Great Depression (grayt dee-PREH-shun)—A time period of economic crisis that occurred from 1929 to 1940 after the stock market crashed on October 29, 1929. Very few people had money. Unemployment was high. People struggled to find enough food to feed themselves and their families.

organization (or-gah-nih-ZAY-shun)—A group of people who come together for a specific purpose.

trust fund—A bank account, often set up for a child, for use when the child becomes an adult.

veterinarian (veh-trih-NAYR-ee-un)—A doctor who works with animals.

INDEX